Better Fishing
Freshwater

John Mitchell

KAYE & WARD · LONDON
in association with Methuen of Australia
and Hicks Smith, New Zealand

First published by
Kaye & Ward Ltd
1968
Revised edition 1978
Reprinted 1983

ISBN 0 7182 1455 2

All enquiries and requests relevant to this title
should be sent to the publisher, Kaye & Ward Ltd,
The Windmill Press, Kingswood, Tadworth, Surrey, and not
to the printer.

Printed in Great Britain by
Fletcher & Son Ltd, Norwich

Contents

Foreword

FISHING is my job and fishing is my sport and, in moving around the country and various parts of the world reporting on angling, I meet thousands of keen fishermen and see many fish caught by successful methods.

Some years ago I became aware that there was much more to the sport of angling than the proverbial 'eighty per cent skill and twenty per cent luck' rule.

Luck does play a part, for how else can one explain the novice angler who lands a specimen or even a record fish.

But note in the angling press how consistent are the names which make the headlines with match-winning catches week after week at the open matches, how the specimen hunters constantly catch big fish, and you will realise there must be much more to fishing than first meets the eye.

There are many points which go towards making a successful angler— a clean and tidy tackle box, with every item of tackle ready for use when needed, landing-net made up and keepnet ready to both land and hold the catch, and bait both fresh and clean.

Perhaps more important than anything is the need to use a sharp hook—sharpened on a fine oilstone or file. A sharp hook is the introduction between angler and fish and this is one first impression which has got to be perfect. The most expensive fishing tackle in the world will fail to catch the fish when the hook is blunt.

These then are some of the reasons I have been happy to write BETTER FISHING and produce the pictures. Most of the pictures were specially taken and a few—to illustrate a vital fact—came from my picture library.

To get you fishing

This is the time of triumph for every angler—the moment when the fish, having been tempted to take the angler's bait, has been hooked and played and is about to slide into the landing net.

And this is what BETTER FISHING is really all about.

These first two pictures show more than the actual landing technique —on the right is the tray holding bait at a convenient height. Next to it is another tray holding the tackle that will be needed to change to a heavier line—the fish is being brought to the landing net by a line which has a breaking strain of only one and a half pounds. There is also the disgorger for removing the hook, a keepnet ready to hold the bream, and the rod-rest.

CASTING

The action of getting the float and bait out to the swim is called casting and on this page and the next, the whole sequence of casting is shown. In these four pictures note how the angler keeps his eye on the float tackle, to make sure it does not get wrapped around the tip of the rod. Make sure when you are casting out the bait that your own position is firm and that you have your balance. And keep it without falling into the water yourself!

The two pictures on this page and the first picture on the next page show the end of the casting sequence. Note how the arms are fully extended. This is the correct method of casting giving extra casting power and reach. In the first picture the finger controls the line as it shoots out from the reel. Should the bait and float be heading in an undesired direction—into a clump of weeds, for instance—the line can be stopped by finger pressure as the rod is lifted away from the snag.

I am certain that too much is made of the whole action of casting. People have tended to make this more difficult than it actually is! Remember there is just one object in casting—to get the bait out to the fish in the swim. If you can keep the rod in front of the body-line and not let it wave behind you like a wand, then the float and bait will always travel before the rod and not tangle up.

You can practise casting in the garden or on the lawn without ever going near a stretch of water until you can cast really well. Put your basket or seat on the grass and place a series of rubber rings at various distances away. (The distances can be measured out in yards to give some idea of your actual casting distance.) Tackle-up with rod, reel, line, float and lead split shot, but leave off the hook as it can snag up in the grass. Hold the rod as in the pictures and try to get the float in the rubber rings. A half hour at this and you should be able to cast like a champion.

The second picture shows the float as it is in the water trotting down to take the bait to the fish. Only the tip is showing because the float is correctly weighted down with lead shot. As the float travels down the swim so the line is tightened – but not too tight – ready for a bite.

PLAYING

The float has dipped and this usually means that a fish has shown interest in the bait. This bite, as it is called, is followed by a movement

from the angler taking the rod in the opposite direction away from the bite—called the *strike*. From now on the action is called 'playing the fish' and, dependent on how the angler 'plays' his catch, is the successful landing of his fish. In other words, play the fish correctly and you have a fish-catch; do the wrong thing—like trying to reel *in* line when the fish wants to *take* line—will usually end in a break with the hook still in the mouth of the fish or the fish frightened so much it will not feed for the rest of the day; probably taking the whole shoal away with it.

A correct strike depends greatly on not having a lot of loose line out between the tip of the rod and the float. This line can sink under the surface of the water and the drag on such a line can be so much as to stop a correct hooking of the fish in the mouth.

As soon as the strike is made, the fish is going to head for the opposite direction and this 'play' is taken up on the rod via the rod-rings (see page 15). The rod is held well up and away from the direction of the run.

Much of the playing of a fish is practical common sense, and is best learned by the waterside with a fish on the end of the line. But note in both pictures on this page how the rod is held well up to take the strain of the fighting fish. Every fish you catch will have some fight in it, even a small minnow, and this fight is part of what anglers call fishing. Take your time–it is all on your side–when you are playing the fish. Don't hurry to get it in the landing net. Keep a tight line between the rod-top and the fish.

If the fish makes a sudden dive towards a weed-bed give it side strain on the rod (see first picture on page 11). In the two pictures on this page, you will note that the angler is holding the rod in his right hand and playing the fish only by the tip of the rod. He is not winding the reel but, should the fish make a run which could be controlled by side strain, the angler would be able to give plenty of line by just pressing the centre of the reel. This reel is called a closed face reel, and line is released by touching the centre. A wind on the reel-arm will take up line instantly. One of the great beauties of this type of reel–the closed face reel–is that

line twist can never occur under most normal fishing conditions and its use is therefore very great for spinning or live-baiting. Many match-anglers use this reel for another reason; one can cast without anything holding back the line – the reel itself as with a centre-pin reel or the bale arm of the normal fixed spool reel.

By now the fish is well played out and tired, ready to be landed, but there is still a chance for it to make a last-minute dive for the safety of the weed-bed. And so the angler now uses his right hand on the handle of the reel, still keeping one finger of the right hand ready to give out line if a lot is needed.

The reel has a 'slipping clutch' mechanism but the fish – as it tires – can be played by direct winding on the reel. The slipping clutch is very useful to help save the line breaking should you not be fast enough to give line yourself and is built in to most fixed spool reels and a few multiplier reels. However, if you can learn to play the fish without using the slipping clutch, you will enjoy more action and better sport from your fishing.

LANDING

The fish which took the bait turned out to be a small roach—it would make an ideal live-bait for pike during the winter—and our angler decided the landing net was not needed to bring the fish to his hands.

Instead of using the net (but always use a landing net for a good fish) the angler decided to swing the fish in. During a fishing match, where the best weight wins the contest, much time can be saved by swinging in the small fish—especially if the match only lasts four or five hours and you are 'pegged' in a known small-fish section.

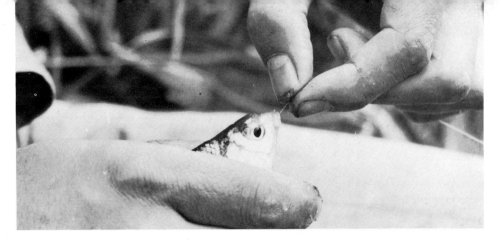

UNHOOKING

Now comes the moment of unhooking the fish. This is an easy job if the fish—as in the picture—is hooked in the top or lower lip. (Incidentally, fast striking, as soon as the float moves in the water, will usually mean the hook will go into the fish on its mouth and not be taken right down.)

The fish is held in one hand and the fingers of the other hold the end of the hook. Taking a firm hold of the hook, turn the fish and the hook will come free. The fish will usually extend its lips (see lower picture) and this helps the action of unhooking.

Should the fish take the hook right down, then a disgorger will have to be used to remove the hook. Place the forked end of the disgorger in the bend of the hook (still holding the fish with the other hand) and hold the line tight to the disgorger (see page 47). Now push down into the mouth turning the hook away from where it is stuck into the fish and this will free the hook. *Do not* pull the hook free—this is cruel and could tear the mouth and injure the fish. Disease can set in and the fish can die. This is not sporting, to say the least.

TACKLE LIST

1. Bait containers.
2. Keepnet.
3. Landing net.
4. Tin of feeder maggots (for catapult).
5. Float and lead shot container.
6. Groundbait container (bait is mixed in this).
7. Seat and fishing basket
8. Dry groundbait can be kept in a canvas water bucket.
9. Loaf of bread for making crust or flake bait.
10. Top of feeder maggot tin used as a sieve.

Note: Every item of tackle, except rod and line with reel, has been put out on the bank ready for use. This angler is a keen matchman and makes a practice of putting his rod, reel, line through rings, float, split shot, and hook up, last of all. 'It pays in better fishing' he says.

ASSEMBLY

Putting the rod together correctly–so that it can also be taken apart with ease–is one of those jobs which we nearly always hurry. If the ferrule is a little bit hard to push on–we try to force it–and then find difficulty in taking the rod apart when we have finished fishing for the day. Take time to make sure the ferrules are clean and free of dirt and, perhaps, sand. Keep them lightly oiled, or better, lightly touched over with a piece of candle grease. When the rod is assembled, check to make sure that the rod-rings are all lined-up correctly. It will save you missing a ring when you are threading through the nylon line. This is important because, if the nylon does miss a ring, the rod will not be able to do its job properly when playing a fish. That job is to take the strain of action from the fish.

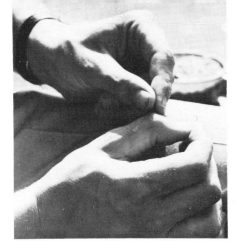
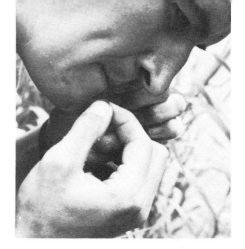

This is one job—tying a size 22 hook—I suggest could be learned better at home than by the riverside. Especially on a cold day in winter when you cannot feel the tips of your fingers. The hook whipping is quite straight forward; given in all nylon and knot-tying cards available freely from tackle shops and can be practised better on a thicker strand of nylon than that used for whipping a size 22 hook (one of the smallest we use).

Sharp teeth are always better for this job—of cutting off the end of the whipping—than scissors.

For fixing lead shot on the line (to sink the float to show only the tip), we only need to pinch it on between fingers. If the shot you are offered in the tackle shop is too hard for this simple operation, do not buy it. Insist on soft lead shot. Split shots are available in many different sizes and a simple rule to remember is to use the size of shot to suit the action you wish to give to the bait.

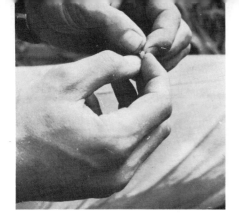

Putting the maggot-bait correctly on the hook is obviously one of the most important things in fishing. Remember to keep the point of the hook needle-sharp—with a fine file or oilstone—squeeze the maggot and put it on to the hook by the blunt end. The maggots—a hook can be loaded with up to six at a time—must be seen to be alive and wriggling. A dead maggot will rarely attract a fish to bite. Before baiting-up a hook when float-fishing, it is important to know how to set the float, so that the bait will just be tripping the bottom, or where to set the float so that the bait is on the bottom of the swim. Both these jobs are done with the aid of a plummet lead. This has a cork inset in which to stick the hook and not cause it to be blunted. The hook is passed through the wire ring of the plummet and then the point is pushed into the cork. If the float sinks, pull it up the line; if it then lies on top of the water there is too much line between float and lead shot, so adjust as needed to only show the tip of the float.

TROTTING

When the float and bait have been cast in and the bait sunk to the required level – this is the job of the lead shots and the faster the bait gets down the better are the chances of contacting a fish – the float has to be watched for a dip, a movement to one side – in fact any indication of a bite. At the end of the swim hold back the float for a couple of seconds. This will have the action of lifting the bait off-bottom and could result in a bite, probably from a dace.

Watching the float with the sun directly shining in your face could result in a headache, so wear a sun shield or better, a pair of 'Polaroid' glasses. (With these glasses you can see to some extent under the surface of the water.)

'Mending' the line does not mean tying knots to join two pieces of nylon together! Slack line on the surface of the water can mean lost bites because the rod-top is not in direct contact with the float and line will have to be taken up on the reel to make a direct strike.

As the float travels downstream it usually goes a fraction slower than the surface speed of the water. This means that the line goes in a 'snake-form' and will have to be straightened out or mended, by lifting the rod and slightly reeling in line. This mending of the line to ensure a direct bite is one of the most important points to *better fishing* and more bites have been lost by having a slack line than by missing the dip of the float.

It is very important to keep the float container close to your basket or seat, in order that a quick change of floats can be made without moving or standing up. The float box seen here is home made and has containers for lead shot, float-caps, lead 'bombs' and everything else needed to make a quick change of terminal tackle. Time saved at this stage must mean more time for tackle in the water and more chances of fish.

You could find that more water is coming downstream than when you first started fishing. This will mean a change of tactics and the faster you do this—without having to clamber up the bank to sort out the needed tackle—the faster you will be taking account of the changed conditions.

When conditions are light—little stream or in still-water fishing—there is no real need to secure the float to the line by having rubber rings or float-caps both top and bottom of the float. Make the float by using one cap only—at the bottom of the float. This will give a far more sensitive bite and have the advantage of almost taking the line direct from rod-top to hook. When using the 'slider-float' tactic—where the float is free to move up the line—the float is 'stopped' by a piece of nylon whipped to the reel line and no caps or rubber rings hold the float in place. In the picture below only the tip of the float is showing. The float is got to this position by carefully weighing it down—or balancing it—by the use of split lead shots.

These four pictures illustrate the angler's catapult in action (another type of catapult is shown on page 32). It is used for getting maggots out to a swim some distance away from the angler and can also be used for taking heavy balls of groundbait out too.

I have never yet been able to buy the right kind of catapult in a fishing tackle shop and so have always made my own. Strong wire for the frame, $\frac{1}{8}$ inch square rubber, nylon line for the rubber-whippings and a piece of leather for the maggot-bag is all that is needed.

Another method of taking maggots, chrysalis (casters) or hempseed grains to the right swim is by a contraption which can be made of an ordinary piece of thick bamboo cane. The cane is hollowed-out to a depth of six inches and filled with bait. It is then 'flicked' to the required swim by holding firmly in the right hand, aiming and pulling back on the top of the cane with the left hand.

As with the float container, the mixing bowl of groundbait is kept close to the angler's seat so that the swim can be fed little and often. The

groundbait is brought to the swim dry and there is mixed with water. Just how stiff you make the groundbait really depends on the conditions of the water. Flowing fast and deep, the bait is made up stiff so that it gets down to the bottom first and then breaks up to attract the fish. When this picture was taken (bottom) the water was flowing slightly and the fish were feeding in a line just off bottom. The bait was mixed light (with very little water added) and broke up almost as it hit the surface. It was made of bread-crumbs mixed with a little custard powder (to give a yellow colour) and cast in little and often. It produced roach. Note that the angler holds the rod in his hand as he casts in the bait.

If the water held good quantities of bream, the bait could have been made stiffer to keep a bream-shoal 'rooted' to the spot. Bream feed very heavily and then move off to find more food. The whole object during a contest—where bream make most of the big weights—is to keep the shoal feeding in front of *your* swim for the whole length of the match.

Bigger and better fishing

This picture contains almost the whole story of fishing! The angler nearest the camera is about to land his fish (a bream). The ring in the centre of the picture comes from a bream which is fighting back after being hooked and can be seen on the surface, while the circle in the top left hand of the picture is produced by a bream biting on the bait to pull the float under. So in one picture we have hooking, playing and landing a fish.

BETTER LANDING

The angler in the centre is being watched by anglers on either side as he lands his fish. The control on the bream is made with the tip of the rod with the line held tight on the reel. The rod is drawn back – bringing the fish nearer – and the landing net is lowered under the surface and pushed towards the fish. Remember to keep the rim of the net under the water.

Having got the fish into the net, lift the net quickly upwards so that the fish is held by the mesh.

Now the angler on the far left is landing his bream. Note that the angler has the rim of his net under and that the fish has naturally gone into the net. The four pictures, on this and the previous page, were a complete sequence and also show the big area that can be covered by members of the same bream-shoal on a canal. Most of the bream were around the same size – an average of three pounds each.

A long-handled landing net is needed when fishing a swim with high banks, or banks that slope with a slight angle towards the river. In the latter condition the water is shallow and the all-important point about lowering the rim of the net under the water-surface is just not possible without the use of a landing-net-handle-extension.

The extensions can be made of cane, but modern practice is to use a metal handle that can be extended by merely pulling out a centre-shaft.

If the fish spots the landing net as it is being drawn towards you, the chances are great that the fish will be frightened even more than it is at being hooked and will probably make one last bid for freedom. This is one of the great dangers to be considered when a friend offers to land a fish for you – and friends love to help you land your fish! But just let a big

fish see or be touched by the landing net held by you or a friend and the chances of a break-away are big. 'Played it right up to the landing net, he did – and then it touched and broke away' is a comment I've heard far too many times!

A short-handled landing net can be used when bank and depth conditions are right. A low bank and enough water to keep the net under and reel in the fish. With the short handle and a heavy fish there is less chance of bending the handle. It is amazing just how much pressure even a pound roach will put on the handle!

As I have explained on page 12, it is quite in order to swing in the small fish – the bleak, dace and gudgeon – when fishing a match. These fish do make a match-weight more; but always have the net ready for use!

When you have got the fish into the landing net, pull the net closer to you and lift well clear of the water. If balanced on the edge of the net the fish can still jump free, break the nylon and get away.

Landing is one of the most important parts of fishing and if you re-member the simple rules of getting the fish into the landing net you should have no trouble.

Do not attempt to land the fish until it is really tired out. With most fish this moment can be seen—it is when the fish lies on its side as it is being played towards you.

Do not have the landing net rim above the surface of the water. The sighting of the net can frighten a fish into making one last bid for freedom. *Sink* the edge of the net under the surface and bring the fish into it by using the tip of the rod with one finger controlling the reel.

Do not push the net into the fish. Rather, as it goes into the net, scoop upwards, and the fish will fall completely into the net.

Once it is in the net, lift completely clear of the water and, if the fish is a specimen, take the net away from the water's edge before starting to remove the hook. As you get more proficient and, especially when match-fishing, you will be able to remove the hook while the fish is still in the net. Hold the catch with the net as you remove the hook, and then slip it into your keepnet.

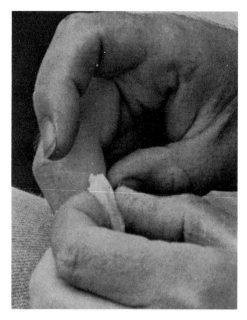 

BREAD BAITS

Bread is the most convenient of all fishing baits and just about the cheapest. It can be used in many different forms—as paste, flake, crust or in cubes—and will be taken by every freshwater fish. Pike even fall for a lump of bread when live-bait is scarce! Bread, because it has been used by anglers for so long, is also a 'natural' bait for fish. The form it is usually presented in is flake. Our first picture shows a piece of soft bread torn off a new loaf being 'moulded' round a hook. Pressure is put on the long shank of the hook and this helps to hold the bread to the hook. If the bread does not fall off when retrieving the float and hook, the bread is far too firm on the hook! Put the amount of pressure on, which will ensure the bread falling off as you wind in.

The second picture shows the angler wetting the bread slightly and biting off the edge so that it hangs perfectly in the water and looks attractive to the fish. By the way, the bait must have been attractive on the day I took this picture—the angler had over 100 lb of very good tench!

30

The hands forming this bait—it is bread with a small amount of cheese mixed in to form a paste—belong to the former roach record-holder, Mr Bill Penney. The roach weighed 3 lb 14 oz and took breadflake bait to a size ten hook fished on the bottom of a reservoir. This should be proof enough that bread is a good bait for the really big fish. Bill once told me that he put bread baits above all others for catching sizeable fish. 'I may take some small redworms along when I go fishing, but I rely mainly on all the forms of bread. And naturally, flake is my favourite.'

MAGGOTS

The next most popular bait—for match-anglers it is *the* most important—is maggots, and in the picture this young angler has found the bait has been 'sucked' without the angler seeing a bite. It could have been wrong shotting (with the float too high in the water) which was responsible for the bite not being noticed. The obvious thing to do—as the angler is doing—is to rebait with maggots and cast out to the same spot. This time watching the float every second for a bite.

GROUNDBAITING

The use of a catapult was explained on page 22 and the picture above (left) shows another type of catapult which is a stronger model and used by matchmen who constantly fish well away from the swim just in front of them.

Groundbait can also be bought in pellet form and these are hard enough to throw by the handfull without first wetting them. Groundbait balls can be made by mixing water with the bait so that it sticks together well and will not break up when in the air. Most of the water is squeezed out when the ball is made. (Matchmen often practise their accuracy in throwing groundbait balls by substituting with tennis balls and a bucket in a field. This is keenness and pays dividends in a match such as the National Angling Championship when this is held on a wide river or drain.)

SWIMFEEDER TACTICS

One method of making sure that the groundbait is near the hookbait is by using the swimfeeder technique. The picture on the left shows the swimfeeder baited up with a mixture of groundbait and maggots. Maggots are the hookbait in this case, but bread could well have been on the hook. The swimfeeder is tied by a small length of nylon to a swivel which is free to travel up the line. It is stopped sliding down to the hook by a small split lead shot pinched to the main reel line above the hook length knot.

The pictures show, top right, a side strike made when the angler was feeder fishing, and, below, an empty open-ended feeder reeled in with a dace on the hook.

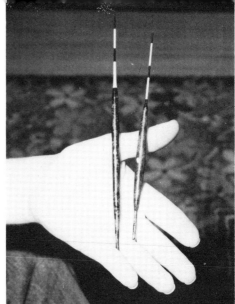

FLOAT-MAKING

It is quite easy to make your own fishing floats and you could find conditions where a shop-bought float will not have the right action. Evening classes on angling make quite a feature of building floats and you will find everyday materials suitable for making floats available in your own home. Floats can be marked to show what lead shot they need to sink and the kind of wind in which they behave best. Use dots or numbers painted on the float or make use of the small 'Letraset' outfits available at stationers.

The bottom picture shows a roach pole in action. It is the length of these 'poles' which is the great attraction. Today they are made of glass fibre and are light. This pole was eighteen feet in length and with it the angler was able to hold his float 'tight'. Poles do not have reels or a moving line and, when a fish is played out, the pole is taken apart to land the fish.

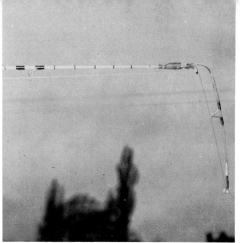

BITE DETECTION

The first three pictures show various methods of determining a bite from a fish. The first is the 'dough-bobbin', probably the most simple and certainly the cheapest method. A small piece of dough or bread is pressed on the line. When it moves or jerks this shows a bite from a fish, and the strike is made. The next is the swing-tip used by tightening up on the line when legering and watching for movement on the tip. It is flexible.

The third picture shows the wire indicator. This is a length of fine wire whipped to the bank-stick and the reel line is rested on the wire to show the slightest bite from a fish.

The last picture shows the tip of the fishing rod under the water to avoid the effect of wind on the line. The angler is float-fishing and the float is connected to the line by the bottom ring only (see page 21). The line between float and rod is kept tight and the bite-indication shows on the float-tip.

CONTROL BY ROD AND REEL

Try if possible to face the sun when fishing. With the sun behind you it is much easier to be seen by the fish. The lower picture shows a fish finally played out and ready for landing (see page 29).

These four pictures all have something in common. The top pictures show control on the reel as the fish is being landed with the rod in the right hand. Below (left) the angler is still fighting his fish and controls the action by a combination of rod and reel movement. The picture on the right shows control and landing of a fish by an angler who is right-handed, but prefers to hold the landing net in his right hand and control the fish with his left hand. (Note the reel-handles are to the left.)

It is important to keep the rod held well up when playing a fish. *Never* point the rod directly at the fish. This could result in the fish breaking free. This angler is playing his catch by holding the rod up and giving or reeling in line as the fish dictates.

Below (left) is the position of the finger, bale-arm open, prior to casting. The rod is lifted, the movement started and the line released as the float or leger weight is cast. Below (right) shows the position of the hands when reeling in line.

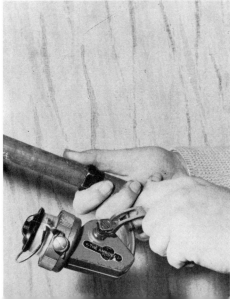

The angler in the above picture is carefully playing his fish on the fixed spool reel. His line has a breaking strain of only just over one pound and the tip-action light rod is well able to take the strain of playing a bream of three pounds. Note that the rod appears to be an extension of the arm—as it should be—and this makes for excellent control. The angler in fact is very experienced and is a member of a match team that fishes the National Angling Championship.

LANDING WITHOUT FUSS

Both pictures on this page show the rim of the landing net under the surface of the water as the fish slides over the rim. It is also important to keep a tight line on the fish and to keep the head slightly out of the water as the fish comes in and over the rim. Providing the landing net is under the surface and the line is kept tight on the fish, it will not notice the net and take fright.

The fish in this picture (above) is fully played out and the picture was taken as the net was being lowered under the surface. Below, the moment to watch as the fish, still held by a tight line, is in the net and being lifted clear of the swim. Try to do this—the landing of your catch—without fuss. Splashing about on the surface has two risks—the fish can be lost by breaking free, and the splashing will certainly frighten other fish away.

Not all landing nets are of the same shape. This one is triangular and instead of a metal rim extending all the way round, it has a nylon rim made of netting nearest the entrance. This almost completely eliminates the possibility of the fish spotting something else is wrong (apart from being hooked!) and taking fright. Such landing nets are most useful where weeds are present, but if you remember the rules of landing your catch (play the fish out fully, sink the edge of the landing net and keep a tight line) you will have no trouble.

Foul hooking a fish does not mean that you have done something against the laws of fishing. It merely means that the fish has not taken the bait in its mouth. Usually what happens when a fish is foul-hooked

(as in the picture above) is that the fish was probably attracted to the bait (this shown by a slight movement on the float or bite-indicator) but then decided to play about with the food. The resulting strike did not take the hook into the mouth but hit some other part on the body. In the picture, the fish–a sea trout taken in a tidal river–was hooked in the tail. The fight from a foul-hooked fish is always more difficult than that from a fish hooked in the mouth. This angler who hooked the sea trout thought at first that he had hooked a big pike!

A faster strike at the very split second of the dip of the float or the indication of the bite, should avoid foul hooking or make it quite rare. As you progress to BETTER FISHING your reaction to the right moment to strike will become very much faster and foul hooking of a fish almost forgotten.

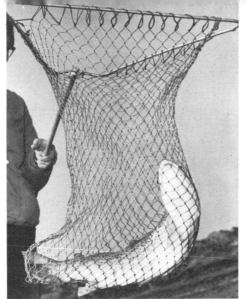

BETTER LANDING NETS

Safely in the landing net, left, is the foul-hooked sea trout, and, right, a 4 lb chub. When buying a landing net aim for one with a wide rim and deep in the net. You will see from the above pictures and also the top picture on the next page that the netted fish sinks right to the bottom of the deep net. With a shallow net the fish could leap for freedom and make it. Remember that once the fish is clear of the water it is out of its natural haunt and will try to return to the water if at all possible. And this is not possible if it is engulfed in a deep landing net.

The fish in the top picture (left) is a bream and at the end of the day the net had a covering of the slime found on most fish. When the angler got home he washed the landing net and his keepnet in cold water to remove the slime. (This, incidentally, helps protect the fish against diseases.)

Right is a trout that has just been netted while the bottom picture shows the angler admiring his catch, a specimen roach. When you catch such a fish and there is a photographer around try to get him to take a picture of you looking at your catch, rather than at the camera.

BETTER UNHOOKING

Never pull the hook straight out of the mouth of the fish. This will cause damage to the fish. If you have a specimen fish—the top picture shows a big bream—unhook it gently by taking a firm hold of both the fish and the hook. With small fish (see page 13) the fish is turned off the hook and with a specimen the hook is turned. The lower picture shows a fish well hooked in the mouth. This fish is a tench and you will find the tench has a strong mouth and that a wet cloth wrapped around the fish will give a better hold when unhooking. The wet cloth will also be better for the health of the fish.

The size of the roach above can be judged by the hand holding it. The roach weighed 2 lb 10 oz and was taken on breadflake fished to a size ten hook used on float tackle.

The angler unhooking a small roach in the lower picture is using a disgorger to remove the hook which has been taken right into the mouth of the fish.

Fine tackle fishing basically means using lines and hooks that are enough to give the fish a sporting chance. But it is not good fishing to use tackle so fine that the fish breaks free and is allowed to trail about with a hook, a length of line and perhaps a float still in its mouth. It is true that a fish will quickly get rid of a broken-off hook but it does hurt the fish. And there is nothing sporting in such action. It is better fishing to balance the strength of tackle with the probable size of fish that can be expected to bite. And then to use your skill in landing the fish. Pike of ten and twelve pounds regularly get landed by anglers using lines of four pounds and below to single maggot baits on a size 16 or 18 hook. As an example of fine fishing, the above anglers are using freshwater tackle fishing from a pier—in the Adriatic!

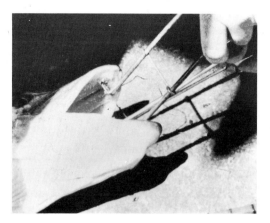

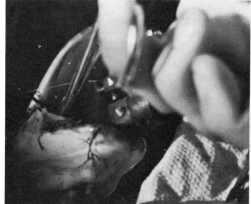

UNHOOKING THE PIKE

Unhooking a pike can present a problem because of the sharp teeth of the fish, but this is easy to overcome by using a gag to hold the jaws apart as the hooks are removed.

The gag has a clamp and to avoid stretching the jaws too much – and hurting the fish – this clamp should be used in place.

A pair of long-nosed pliers or strong artery forceps (these can be bought from an ex-service supply store) can be most useful when unhooking a pike to save your fingers accidentally brushing against its needle-like teeth.

Providing you have made the strike at the right moment – after the first run when the fish has stopped to turn the bait in its mouth – the treble hook should be firm in the side of the pike's mouth. Open the mouth with your fingers, using the gag to keep open if needed, hold the hooks with the pliers, and push slightly into the mouth to free. As with other actions in fishing it is much harder to describe than to do.

TAKING MEASUREMENTS

Better fishing will mean bigger and better catches. And naturally, before returning the fish to the water to live and fight again, you will want to have a record of the catch. It should be weighed accurately on a good spring balance (hold the fish in a plastic bag while doing this and not by the gills!). It can be measured by taking the exact distance round the fish (the girth) at the 'thickest' part and by measuring the length from nose or mouth to the tip or fork of the tail (record which measurement you take on a rough drawing). If the specimen is a dace or a roach and you wish to enter the catch for a newspaper competition (see later in the book) you will have to take a couple of scales from the 'shoulder' of the fish. The scales are best lifted off with a sharp penknife and put straight into an envelope or film negative bag. Make sure to mark the envelope with the details of the fish and where the scales came from and include the weight, girth, length, where caught and when. Nothing is more frustrating than having a pair of fish-scales and not knowing from what fish they came and where and when!

AND A PICTURE

Naturally you will want to take a picture of your catch – to go with the other recordings – to send in to support a claim for a competition and to show your friends the kind of fish you catch.

Try to include something in the picture in order to establish the size of your catch. For instance, in the second picture I have included a normal matchbox to show its size in relation to that of the roach. All these were specimen roach ranging between 1 lb 12 oz and 2 lb 10 oz in size. (I stress a normal size matchbox because you *can* get miniature matchboxes!)

Try also to be as quick as possible when taking the picture as fish do suffer when kept out of water too long. Get the camera ready – with the film set to take – before getting the fish out of the keepnet; and have an idea of the type of picture or shot you are going to take. After the button is pressed put the fish back quickly into the keepnet or into the water.

MY WAY WITH PICTURES

I often get asked how to take good angling pictures; usually when I am taking a picture and haven't really got time to explain fully.

I have the time now but, before I explain, let me stress that this is how *I* take a picture. (I mention this because when I suggested that a friend, who is the best angler I know and who is also a great writer and photographer, write on *his* photography in a magazine, he was pounced upon by other camera-users and told that the same effect could be produced on much cheaper equipment. All the time he was merely stating how *he* did it—and this is what I want to do. At the same time, you do not *have* to use an expensive camera to produce a good angling picture of your catch).

Angling pictures generally fall into two main types. The two pictures, on this and the preceding page, show the factors required. The first picture (on page 52) is an action shot of an angler about to bring his catch in and, as the subject was moving, the camera needed a fast speed to 'freeze' the action. The finished photograph also shows a 'pictorial' scene and, so to keep the foreground, subject and background in focus, the 'f' setting was made small. The camera was set to take the picture at a speed of 1/125 second at an aperture of f 16.

The focus was made on the angler and the camera 'set' before the angler caught his fish. Even so, the speed setting could have been higher (at 1/500 second or 1/250 second) as there is still a little movement on the fish, but some photographers would argue that as the shot is an action picture there should be a little movement to show this.

The second picture (on page 53) shows an angler holding a fine barbel up to the camera. Here there is no movement and the picture was a record of the catch (the same as I hope you will be taking). The picture had to show the fish (see how the scales show cleanly and can almost be counted) and the captor. The background did not really matter, as it did in the other picture, and in fact is slightly out of focus. The camera was set on an aperture of f 11 with a speed of 1/60 second and focussed on the fish. (Depth of field – the depth at which the picture is still sharp – at f 11 is enough to include both angler and fish.)

For both pictures and for most of the pictures in this book I use a film called TRI X. This is a very 'fast' film and I need it because I generally take pictures at the end of the day when the light is not so strong as at midday. The film is developed in D 76 or ID 11 developer. Also for the record, I use Rollieflex twin lens reflex cameras on the $2\frac{1}{4}$ inch square format film. I also use cameras of the 35 mm format, Leicas, Nikon and Olympus because of wide angle and telephoto lenses that can be changed when needed. The pictures of the angler fishing on the Thames with people swimming alongside was taken with a Leica camera and a 35mm lens. The lens was set at f5·6 to give sufficient depth of field and the shooting speed was 1000th of a second to catch this action. The angler incidentally did not appear to notice all the other sports going on around him and in fact won his club match with a catch of sizeable dace. The picture, taken during a bank holiday, was used across half the front page of Angler's Mail. There was no movement in the scene of the other picture which illustrates fishing on the Thames across the river from the Houses of Parliament and near Lambeth Bridge. To get the depth of field the 28 mm lens on the Olympus camera was set at f11 and used at 1/60 of a second. I know this camera equipment is expensive, but remember I have to earn a living partly from taking photographs that are reproduced in newspapers and, because the pictures

are printed on newsprint, the quality has to be about one third better than photographic reproductions.

If by now you are looking at your own camera which may not have focussing knobs and settings to alter the aperture or speed and are wondering if you can take good angling pictures, let me tell you the answer is *Yes*.

My object here was to work with the reflections in the water to build up a colourful picture as the angler netted a pike that had taken minnow bait. The picture was shot at 125th of a second (there was little 'action' that had to be stopped) and the lens closed to f11 to give depth. Focus was on the landing net by the angler's hand.

PICTURE POINTS TO WATCH

There are a few things to watch but you can still produce a good picture and – more important – a record of your catch without the need for an expensive camera. The first picture (on page 52) could have been taken easily with a 'set-speed-set-focus' camera from the same position as I

have taken my picture. Make sure that the moving fish is coming towards the camera. This will 'freeze' the movement much better than if the fish was moving from left to right.

Taking the angler-holding-the-fish is easy if you remember not to get too close and yet not too far away from the subject. The same rule is true of taking a picture of the catch – try not to go too near the fish. If your camera has a 'flash' attachment, use it when the light is poor or when the sun is strong (throwing shadows into the eyes) to 'balance out' those shadows.

Remember to have the camera ready with film in it and set for action before you take the fish out of the water. And finally, you can take more than one picture (perhaps the angler closed his eyes just as you pushed the button) and if the picture is required to send to a newspaper competition, use black and white film, not colour.

HOLDING THE CATCH

Keepnets, for holding your catch until the end of the day, come in all shapes and sizes. I dearly wish that all anglers would start their fishing life with the largest possible keepnet.

Too many fish crammed in a small net means that some may die because of lack of space to move about in the net. and if you get small and big fish in the same net the big ones will usually be at the top of the net and the small fish at the bottom – and the small fish in particular will suffer as the net is lifted out of the water.

One of the mysteries of fishing is that you can never be quite sure that your next bite is not going to be a British record fish. Or when you will have a day when every cast will produce a big fish. Nothing is worse than not having a keepnet big enough to take all the fish you catch.

Make sure the fish are comfortable inside the net and that the net is well under the water. Also make sure the keepnet is firmly held by the bank stick so that the weight of fish does not sink the net and allow the fish to escape. This net in the picture above is being made more comfortable by the angler lifting it out of the water, straightening it, and then replacing it. The net holds fifty pounds of bream and the angler was catching fish so fast in a contest that he needed two keepnets to contain his catch. This could happen to you. So be prepared!

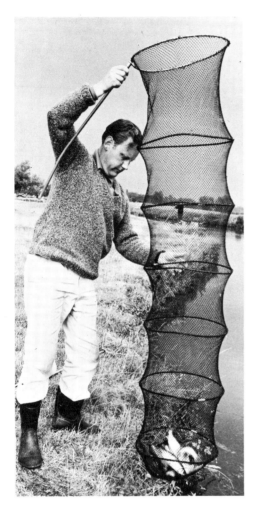

   As I wrote earlier, a big keepnet should be used to hold a catch and the one on the left is by no means too long to allow the catch a free movement. The perch catch in the keepnet in the right picture above were weighed in and returned alive—happy after spending a few hours in the large net.

The chub in the keepnet in the top picture weighed over four pounds and it has plenty of room to move about while waiting to be weighed for the record.

FISH STUDY

When we are fishing it is sometimes hard to imagine what fish are doing under the surface as they search for food. Looking at fish can often give us a clue to how they live and in the picture below and the one on the next page we see how a pike lies in wait for its prey and how perch move among weeds looking for food. Both pictures were taken in a zoo aquarium–perhaps the best place to watch fish in their natural surroundings.

RETURNING YOUR CATCH

When you return your catch, don't throw the fish into the water as
though it were a lump of coal. Such cruelty will harm fish and could kill
some of the bigger specimens. In this picture the angler is returning a
roach which weighed only a couple of ounces under the magic two
pound mark. The fish was exhausted–it needed time to revive after
being in a keepnet for the few hours of the match–and so the angler held
it by the sides in an upright position until it was able to swim away under
its own strength. The same was true of the bream, the barbel and the
pike in the pictures on the next page.

All three fish had fought well and were tired. They needed to be

returned to the water in almost as good a condition as they were when landed and this was not a task to be hurried.

For the sake of your future sport—because you never know if or when you will catch the same fish again—take time to return your catch and if possible hold the head of the fish facing the direction of the stream. So that the water flows into the face or mouth of the fish.

Barbel are especially strong fighters, but it is surprising how quickly the fight fades. If kept in a keepnet on a hot day in summer it is possible for a barbel to feel the strain of being restricted and it could die. Keep an eye on the fish in the net and if it looks uncomfortable, return it to the water—making sure all is well first. I am sure that if you were fishing in a contest, the scalesman would weigh that fish for you, and make a note of its weight, so that you could return it alive to the water.

BETTER FISHING IN ALL WEATHERS

Both anglers in these pictures caught fish although the sun was shining and the water was very clear. They also took advantage of the weather to do a spot of sunbathing. On days like these sport can often seem slow right at the height of the sun. The weather calls for fine tackle, small hooks and small baits—and above all, quietness from the angler.

For the record, the angler in the top left picture with his net full of very good roach fished with a size twenty-two hook tied to one and a half pounds breaking strain line and the reel line had a breaking strain of two pounds. Bait was a single chrysalis allowed to sink slowly by having a very small lead shot about 18 inches away from the hook. He was fishing a canal and had plenty of cover from the fish by weeds lining the sides of the canal.

When the weather is bad try to keep dry and warm with good rainwear. Rubber boots will keep out water and the inner shoes which are available with warm stockings will keep your feet and legs warm even during ice and snow. An angler's umbrella is a 'must' for all-year round fishing. Fish will continue to feed when there is ice on the surface and in fact they will feed much better when there is also moving water under the ice.

NATURE—YOUR FRIEND

It is natural for swans and their young to live on the river. The fish know this and take very little notice. Some anglers however try to frighten swans and other birds away by throwing stones. This of course is noticed by the fish and they too are soon frightened away. On the other hand, try not to feed the swans because this also causes a gathering which is unnatural and gets noticed by the fish!

If you see a group of waterbirds coming down the river, wait until they have passed before groundbaiting the swim.

When cattle stand in the river to drink the movement of their feet disturbs the mud and this action releases quantities of fine food contained in the mud. Fish know this and are to be found actually looking for food (bloodworms and other small forms of water-life) around the legs of the cattle. Fish are used to cattle drinking from the river day after day so, when the cattle move away, try fishing the spot where they have been drinking and you could get a pleasant surprise with a specimen fish. If you are wearing rubber boots, stand in the water-drink and fish close in. You are sure that you will not sink any deeper than have the cattle and that the ground under a shallow layer of water and mud is quite firm.

ASK ADVICE

Never be afraid to ask advice from an adult who is fishing alongside. If you approach in a courteous and respectful manner there are very few senior anglers who will not answer your questions. Some adults will go out of their way to help youngsters understand the sport better. People like Frankie Vaughan, who, when I took this picture, was by the waterside to present prizes in a boys' fishing match. Frankie is a very keen all-round angler and loves coarse, game and sea fishing. When he is asked to appear in a show one of the first questions he asks is 'Where is the nearest fishing and what has sport been like?'

BLEND WITH THE BACKGROUND

Try to blend with the background, so that you do not appear to stand out like a beacon to the fish. If the fish see you or hear you, they will take fright. The top left-hand picture shows an angler firmly set in a 'tree-swim' and he even has an umbrella to keep off the rain. This helps to provide a background in keeping with his position.

The top right-hand picture is of two young anglers sitting quietly and wearing clothing which also blends with their background. Note how the rod-rests are low in the ground—just clearing the water-weeds at the edge of the river.

The angler in the bottom picture has very little natural cover but he is making use of the reservoir wall and is wearing a stone-coloured jersey to help disguise him from the fish. Note how the keepnet is placed well in the water, to hold the catch comfortably.

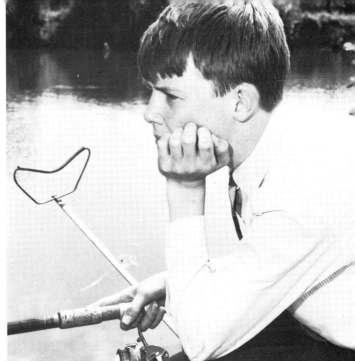

CONCENTRATE

Concentration is one of the great assets of the sport because the angler must know just when the fish has taken his bait in order to make the strike. A late strike will usually mean a missed fish and sometimes this bite could have come from the best fish of the day. If you have not seen the exact moment of the bite and been unable to give a strike, you will never know what you have missed.

The first picture shows a young angler concentrating on the 'dough-bobbin' type of bite-indicator (see page 35) and was taken during a junior fishing match. For the record, the concentration of this angler must have been perfect as a half hour after I took this picture he had a run from a carp, hooked the fish and won the match!

The second picture shows an angler concentrating on watching his float as it travels downstream. He has a rod-rest, but prefers to watch the float taking the fish to the bait. Again, the picture was taken during a match in which this angler did land a prize.

Perhaps the one time not to ask advice from an adult is when he is busy fishing a match. The top picture was taken during a contest on a water that was very clear and the competitors would not have welcomed questions.

Canoes often come between angler and float on canals and there is very little worth doing to upset the boating fans. Remember they have a much right to use the river as we anglers. And to the fish it is quite normal to have such movement as it seems natural.

FISHING IS FUN

Never forget that fishing is *fun* and even though match-fishing calls for concentration and planning it is still a sport and is still *fun*. Matches are organised in which the whole family can take part and of course there are other matches for junior anglers only.

Read the angling press for details of these and your local newspaper probably has a fishing column in which information about matches is given. There is a Junior National Angling Championship staged every year and most fishing associations and angling clubs organise fishing matches for younger members and newcomers to the sport.

Trout Fishing

Since the first edition of BETTER FISHING – FRESHWATER was published a whole new branch of the sport has been enlarged and opened up to the fishing public. This is fly fishing for trout on enclosed waters – man-made lakes and reservoirs – built for water-supply by the regional water authorities and well-stocked by them. These fisheries are run on a day-ticket principle – in some cases there are season ticket arrangements – and on the put-and-take basis. Nearly all trout fisheries have a fish limit which varies between two and eight fish per ticket and a note is kept of every catch. This is used for re-stocking purposes and supplies of sizeable stock fish, which come from trout farms, are usually introduced in the opening months of the season. The trout fishing season normally starts in April or May and lasts about six months according to area.

The two varieties of trout stocked in enclosed fisheries are brown and rainbow trout and under the pellet feeding system used in trout farms can grow big. All are over the size limit of twelve inches and some are very large as in the picture on Page 77 which shows a 13 lb rainbow being introduced to a fly-only trout lake.

The vast majority of fish stocked in these waters are rainbow trout as these are far easier to breed and grow to size quickly. And when in the reservoir or enclosed waters last for around three years–sometimes sooner–before turning into 'dark' or old fish. If after catching a few rainbow trout you contact a 'brownie' you will soon know the diference by the fight. Rainbow trout fight very hard when first hooked, but a brown trout will struggle every inch of the way to the landing net.

Reservoir tackle is used—a rod that is able to cast well—a reel loaded with a suitable fly line and backing to allow for the run of a big fish, and a tapered cast. It is important that the reel and line balance the rod and lines are numbered according to the rod to be used. As most trout fishing is beneath the water surface a sinking line is used. This can be a fast sinker—for deep water sport—a slow sinker or a tip-only sinker for fish feeding just below the surface. Some waters have both an early-morning and late afternoon rise when only flies fished on the surface will attract—fool is perhaps a better word!—and so a floating line is used to help present the fly on the surface.

The angler new to fly fishing is going to be confused by the number of artificial flies or lures that are available or can be seen in a vast library of books on the subject. There are many, many thousands of patterns in a variety of colours and materials and all have names. But as a start let me suggest that during the opening months of a season dark flies tied to a selection of hooks—from size 8 to 14—will catch fish. You will find that trout anglers in particular are very open about what pattern and size of fly they used to 'kill' a fish. They are nowhere as secretive about the successful fly as many coarse anglers can be about their baits and methods.

A lot of useful information can be obtained from other anglers fishing the trout water and of course from local tackle shops who will be keen to show you their ranges of tackle and selections of trout flies. And when you get on in the sport you may find that tying your own flies will be a great interest—especially during the close season months. In trout fishing there is hardly a greater satisfaction than in tying your own pattern and then catching a fish on the fly. The pictures on the preceding pages show the results of BETTER FISHING—for trout.

Better fishing—the results

The pictures so far in this book BETTER FISHING have tried to show how to go fishing for freshwater fish and how to improve your sport by newer methods of catching fish. The pictures that follow show the results of being a good angler, able to take note of conditions, to use your tackle to catch specimen and good fish. The pictures you will now see show catches taken at the end of the day, just before the captors returned their fish to the water. The fish are specimens and every one should contain a ray of hope for every young angler who reads this book.

Remember, when the bait is under the water and a fish is attracted to that bait, the fish—it could be a good fish, a specimen fish or a British record fish—has no means at all of knowing who has presented that bait. It could be an adult or the very youngest of anglers and the fish would still not know who held the rod and tackle. The fish merely looks upon what we call bait, as food. That and nothing else matters to the fish.

What does matter is what you do when you have a bite from a fish. Strike too fast and you will pull the bait from the mouth of the fish and probably scare it. Strike too slow and the chances are that you will miss the fish. Strike at the right moment and the fish is yours to fight and play and land.

ROACH

Fishing for roach is by far the most popular sport with freshwater anglers and a catch like the one shown on the next page would be the dream-catch for many anglers who are forced to fish in small-fish canals where an eight ounce fish is considered a specimen.

The catch is held in the scales-pan ready for weighing and the average weight of each roach is 1 lb 12 oz. The roach were caught on a day when the sun was strong and the water very clear; and the angler had to use very fine tackle and small bait to tempt each fish.

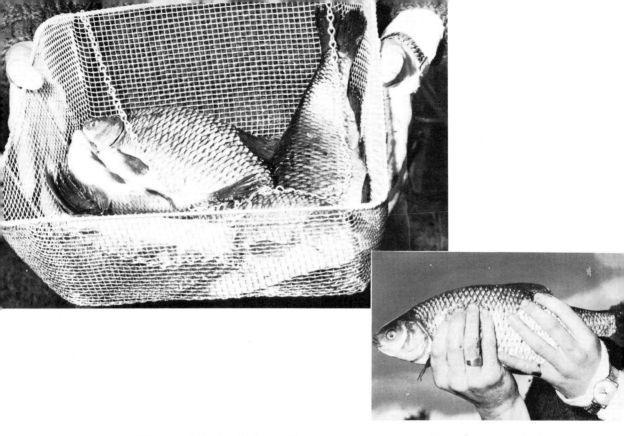

The roach being held up for the camera was the best of the catch shown on the left and it weighed just two pounds.

When fishing for roach the angler has to use tackle to suit conditions of the fishery. If the water is fast and coloured he can use worm or breadflake to a size ten hook and four pound breaking strain line. If the river has slight colour and medium flow, a size sixteen hook to two and a half pounds line and maggots could be suitable. And under clear conditions, where the fish can be seen darting out from weedbeds to grab each piece of food as it falls, the angler uses fine tackle—one and a half pounds b.s. line, eighteen, twenty or size twenty-two hooks and single maggot, chrysalis or wheat baits. He keeps out of sight of the fish and makes as little noise or movement as he can on the bank. Under such conditions it pays to remove the float—or keep it very light and small—and use dust shot to take the bait and hook down to the fish. Groundbait may be used only lightly—cloudbait rather than heavy pudding lumps of groundbait.

BREAM

Bream make most of the big weights in fishing matches and these fish feed mainly on the bottom. They can be seen 'rolling' near the surface at times but the general feeling is that when they are 'rolling' they are not feeding – and they have to be attracted to feed on the bottom so that we can extract them one by one from the swim.

The angler in the picture on the left is seen netting a bream. Note his large keepnet and the various baits. By the way, he is left-handed and the reel handle is on the right. In the picture on the right a fisheries official is putting a bream of 13lb in a river as stock.

Getting the fish to feed on the bottom is quite simple. We put a scattering of groundbait there and when the fish are feeding – bubbles will be noticed on the surface – we merely have to put our hookbait on the same area.

This can be done by legering (a drilled lead 'bullet' or 'bomb', see page 20), or by using a swimfeeder (see page 33). Groundbait may be wrapped around the leger and carefully cast to the groundbait area.

This area need not be large. Try putting the bait in a straight line running parallel to the bank and remember that unless the water has no flow the bait will not sink in a straight line. The faster the flow, the greater will be the angle of fall of the bait. It is important to know exactly where your groundbait is lying because it is there that the bream will be feeding—not where you have first cast your tackle.

Typical bream swim on a canal is shown in the above picture. The angler at first had trouble with floating weed but managed to clear it away from in front of his swim with a landing net. There was not more than five feet of water and fishing with bread to a size ten hook on float tackle the angler managed to extract nearly fifty pounds of bream to 4 lb each during a summer match. Incidentally his clothes and hat blended in with the background and the bank behind him.

CRUCIAN CARP

The smallest true member of the carp family is the crucian carp which is deeper in the body than the common carp and has no barbels on its mouth. Note the long dorsal fin (top fin on the back). This fish weighed over four and a half pounds and was only a few ounces short of the British record fish. It came from a Surrey lake and took two maggots

fished on the float to a size sixteen hook. I made arrangements for it to be given to the London Zoo where it can be found in the Aquarium.

TENCH

The picture on the right shows a tench weighing over four pounds. This fish took breadflake fished on a float-leger tackle, also in a lake. The eye of the tench is small and red and two tiny barbels can be found on the side of the mouth. It is with the help of these barbels that tench find their food.

CARP

This is one of the few times in the sport that you can use two rods and pay attention to them most of the time. This is carp fishing with a bread bait on one hook and partly-boiled potato on the other. Sometimes the bait is a mixture of cat food with other ingredients which is kept a close secret to 'members of the carp syndicate'. One angler I know even keeps the details of his carp bait secret from his wife in case she is questioned by other anglers about his fishing methods! But working on the basis that fish in general will accept any food liked by humans that can be put on a hook it is not hard to experiment with various baits. Incidentally I have found that while some baits provide exceptional catches for a time the fish finally get used to them and so another 'secret' bait has to be found. And then it is back to stage one again!

BARBEL

This barbel of eight pounds took small redworm bait used on swim-feeder tackle when the river was flowing very fast and very coloured. It was one of two fish that the captor–a 16-year-old angler–took to win him the Thames championship title. 'I've never landed a barbel before–but I go to an angling evening class and the teacher there told me the swim-feeder tactics to use' he told me.

The barbel were caught fishing close to the side of a deep swim (the current was too fast to keep the leger right out in the middle of the river except with a heavy lead) and the swim-feeder, loaded with bread-crumbs, put the bait and held it where it could be found by the fish.

When you meet conditions of heavy flood, don't think the fish will not be feeding and just give up. Present your bait out of the strong current–keep the bait big so that the fish can see or find it–and wait for a bite.

85

This eight pound barbel came from a fast-flowing river and fell to luncheon meat bait fished on the bottom close to the edge of the river. The angler found his swim, baited it with pieces of the meat during the day and started fishing just as it was getting dark. He continued in several sessions and caught barbel weighing up to 12 lb from the swim. He also carefully cleared the swim after fishing so that there was no trace that he had enjoyed a good night's fishing. This helped keep the exact location secret until the fish moved to take up spring and summer locations in the river. But every winter the big barbel move back to feed.

PIKE

The biggest freshwater fish you are likely to meet is the pike and this fish in the picture weighed twenty pounds – under half that of the British record fish! After October, the start of the general pike fishing season, you can expect real fun and games when you hook even a small pike. Methods include both live and dead bait fishing, spinning, trolling and even worm-fishing in the sink-and-draw style.

With its long jaws, sharp teeth (see page 49) and deep-set eyes, the pike looks a tough fish to fight and with the weight on its side can give a strong fight. But remember, the pike is there to do a job – to keep down sick and dying fish. It feeds on them and this is natural for the balance of waterlife in a fishery.

Because it looks so tough, don't feel this is a good reason for killing it when on the bankside. If you kill pike and take them home (perhaps for eating, but usually for the cat!) you will not be able to have sport fishing for those same pike. Return your catch, after perhaps taking a photograph to show your friends, and the fish will continue to grow and give more sport to you and other anglers.

Just to prove there is more than one way to land a fish I have included these two pictures of a pike which took live-bait (a small roach) used in a reservoir. In the picture on this page the pike *looks* as though it is about to bite the hand that caught it. Of course this is not really what happened because the fish would not be able to understand that the bait it took (which it looked upon as food) had any connection with the hand. What really happened was that the angler was going to tail the pike (to lift it out by its tail) but the pike had not fully tired and made a last-minute break for freedom.

I would point out that the angler was helping to clear the reservoir of pike because it was to be stocked with trout and the pike present in the water would eat the small trout, if they had not been removed. The

second picture shows that the angler then changed his mind about tailing the fish and lifted it clear by holding the fish just behind the gills.

The pike and perch seen in the third picture are dead. They too came from the reservoir that was being cleared and the fish were eaten. It is rare now for reservoirs to be cleared and the pike and perch killed. Usually the fish are put into other waters that need predatory fish to keep a balance of fish-life.

This preserving of the balance is the main job of pike and I can name many waters where both big pike and big roach live together. Take away the pike in numbers and the roach will quickly breed to a lower average weight. The same is true if the roach are taken away—the pike will gradually get smaller. So a balance of nature is really needed.

One of the most exciting and sporting methods of catching small pike—up to ten pounds—is by a lip-hooked minnow and light tackle. Minnows are first caught in a plastic trap baited with pieces of bread and kept alive and fresh in a bait-kettle. I use a light rod, a fixed spool reel loaded with 4 lb breaking strain line, a float just large enough to support the bait with a couple of lead shots on the line just above the minnow and a small treble hook. The minnow is lip-hooked on the top lip to one of the hooks and all three points are sharpened. As these smaller pike are often found in shallow water, where possible I wade and trot down the float tackle to the waiting fish with the minnow set just off the bottom.

The pictures below show side strain—to turn the head of a pike on the run—and top strain, to lift it away from the bottom.

1. Fresh-caught minnow
2. Lip-hooked on a treble
3. Finding the swim
4. Playing the pike
5. Netted!
6. Lifted clear

Competition fishing

As you progress with your fishing you may decide that you wish to be a member of an angling society–to compete in fishing matches and to enjoy the companionship of other anglers on the club outings and at meetings–or become a member of a specimen fish hunters group.

In both types of club you will find fishing information freely passed between members at meetings and on the river bank.

The one exists to foster angling companionship and catch better match-weights and the other seeks specimen fish. In both you will learn about, and catch, better fish in a shorter time than if you went solo fishing.

When you catch bigger and better fish, be they dace, roach, carp or pike, you may win a club cup for the catch, gain satisfaction as a successful specimen hunter, or win a prize rod or reel in a newspaper competition.

A number of weekly National, Daily, Sunday and local weekly newspapers now give prizes for the best fish entered in their fishing competitions. The rules for entering these competitions are generally the same. The specialist angling newspapers print entry forms and include them in the paper, but the Sunday and Daily newspapers that have contests like an entry in the following manner:

Species of fish . . . Date of capture . . . Name of river or lake . . . Where situated . . . Bait used (if fly state type) . . . Type of rod or reel . . . Method caught (state float, leger, spinning) . . . Line (state breaking strain) . . . Full name of angler . . . Address . . . Telephone No. (if any) . . .

The general rules are as follows. Fish must be caught by fair angling on rod and line. No fish must be caught during the legal close season for the species eligible for the competition. Entries of roach of two pounds and over and dace of three-quarters of a pound and over must be accompanied by two scales from the shoulder of the fish. (Unless this is done the fish could have been a rudd instead of a roach, and a small chub instead of a dace. The scales on fish have different markings according to the species.) *All* entries must be witnessed by two witnesses who must sign a declaration giving their name and address. Witnesses of junior entries (that is from anglers under 16 years) must include at least one adult.

The fish you catch could not only be a specimen but also establish a new national record for its species. I mentioned previously that, when a fish sees your bait in the water, it looks upon it as food and has no means of knowing that the angler (it does not even know an angler is connected with the food) is experienced, slightly keen or out on his or her first-ever trip. If the food is attractive to the fish it will bite; if the food has been badly presented or the fish scared by heavy footsteps or stamping on the bank, the fish will probably not bite. It is as simple as that!

If you are reasonably sure that the fish you have in the keepnet is a record-breaker, (a list of up-to-date British record fish can be obtained free of charge by writing to the National Anglers' Council, 5 Cowgate, Peterborough PE1 1LR, enclosing a stamped and self-addressed envelope.

All record fish are approved by the British Record (rod-caught) Fish Committee at the address above (Phone Peterborough (Code 0733) 54084 during the day or Peterborough 252428 during the evening). The Committee must be informed at once of the catch.

The fish must be weighed accurately on steelyard scales that give the weight in pounds, ounces and drams and these scales must be available for checking afterwards. Witnesses must sign a declaration that you caught the fish by fair angling means and the body of the fish must be made available should the committee or its representative wish to see it. (This is the one time you do not return a fish!)

There are two excellent weekly angling newspapers from which you will get news of the latest catches, fishing matches and other information. Both papers feature special articles for beginners and young anglers and have fish-competitions for anglers under sixteen years of age.

The newspapers are Angling Times and Angler's Mail both published every Wednesday.

Sometimes a specialist angling publication will have a Notable Fish List and at the end of the year or season will award prizes for the best fish caught.

The standard of fish entries is very high and the minimum weights for fish submitted are: Barbel, 10 lb; Carp, 20 lb; Chub, 5 lb 8 oz; Common Bream, 7 lb; Crucian Carp, 2 lb 4 oz; Dace, 14 oz; Eel, 4 lb; Grayling, 2 lb; Perch, 3 lb; Pike, 25 lb; Roach, 2 lb 8 oz; Rudd, 2 lb 8 oz; Salmon, 25 lb; Sea-trout, 8 lb; Tench, 5 lb 8 oz; Brown Trout (river, fly-only), 4 lb; Brown Trout (lake and reservoir, fly-only), 6 lb; and Brown Trout (river or lake, artificial or natural bait), 8 lb.

Index

Fish picture index